T0065617

EYE FOR DETAILS

EYE FOR DETAILS

Prepare to join corporate world

RAJIVA SHARMA

PARTRIDGE
A Penguin Random House Company

Print information available on the last page.

You may reach the author at:

rajiva_s_2000@yahoo.co.uk

To order additional copies of this book, contact
Partridge India
000 800 10062 62
orders.india@partridgepublishing.com

www.partridgepublishing.com/india

CONTENTS

Areas of Attention

Personal Experiences

To
my wife, Rashmi, a persuasive motivator
who knows that I know that
if I can speak, I can write too.

INTRODUCTION

The current century is the century of knowledge. With the Internet revolution, the availability of enormous information is good, but sometimes, when it is contradictory, it causes confusion also, especially in the minds of younger and less-experienced executives. The customer, either internal or external, is restless and expects results yesterday. *Yes* as in *yesterday*. In the bargain, the supplier is under heavy pressure of time. He/she doesn't know how to prioritize. Everything is urgent, and everything is important. This is their everyday routine.

A youngster is fully buried in the stress of life—extended working hours, long travel from residence to workplace, neglecting the young family and elderly parents, etc. This has resulted in increased domestic quarrels, divorces, split families, and sometimes, even suicides.

This concise book has been written purely on my experience to look into certain aspects in advance which could reduce stress and to orient and guide the budding executives who are at the starting point of the corporate ladder. Senior managers may not find it interesting because either they know all what is written or have had different successful experiences. However, the contents here may tell them that they already knew what is written but have been overlooking them because of various reasons. The book is in two parts: one where I have tried to explain certain important areas which if addressed on time can lead to reduced tension-creating causes, and another one is the set of small real-life cases summed up with lessons drawn by me. I am touching up only on the common, non-technical problems of general nature which will remain unchanged and will not make any difference with the method of doing the business. The problems can be handled successfully in many different ways. We may decide the solution of a problem based on the inputs and their analysis. There is nothing called a right or wrong solution; it is your own decision and evaluation as you see it. If you succeed, you are smart, but if you don't, you gain experience. So either way, you are a winner.

A deliberate effort has been made not to link any two chapters. They are independent modules and can be read in isolation.

AREAS
OF
ATTENTION

1

Unlearning

Everyone says, 'Oh, the new-generation kids are smarter than us.' Our parents used to say the same thing for us. Our children also say their kids are so fast that before reaching the age of two years, they can operate an iPad. Well we couldn't operate an iPad and an iPhone in our younger age because Steve Jobs was also from our generation and had not designed Apple gizmos. It is because the children are exposed with an open brain, with enough storage capacity for new knowledge. It is not attributed to continuous improvement in the capacity and quality of the brain generation after generation but talking lightly it is because the young brain does have plenty of unused memory space in it. Therefore, to my mind it is important at all ages to keep unlearning throughout as a routine practice. Obsolete and irrelevant information like old technologies, old schools of thoughts, and bad personal experiences should be forgotten at the earliest after saving the summary of lessons learnt from them. This will create enough clear space available in the brain and thus facilitate faster learning. The extent of unlearning activity varies from person to person.

2

LEARNING

Learning has to be focussed based on your long term carrier plan. I feel creative thinking – people call it out of the box solutions; and sometimes not following the beaten track gives you different and surprising positive results. Learning is not by collecting academic qualification but is by understanding the various equations of how things happen. In any organisation technology is handled by the specialists of the field while overall system is managed by the general managers. In the lighter context, when you start knowing more and more about less and less things till you know everything about tending to nothing you become a specialist. On the contrary when you know less and less about more and more things till you are tending to know nothing about everything you become a manager who is the driving force of any organisation.

We learn from *dos* and *don'ts*, successes and failures. Success makes us move forward, while failures make us more mature. So to my understanding, both add value to our overall personality building. A person is incomplete and weak if he has only seen success and has never failed. We only praise and hail a successful person but don't ever try to appreciate the dark and deep woods he has passed through. A person can never be an entrepreneur if he has not been seasoned on the challenging path. The biggest tasks in business are arranging finances and marketing products on time for smooth cash flow. I have seen many firebrand CEOs who have decided to leave their lucrative jobs and tried to venture into their own businesses fall flat on their faces and fade out into thin air, not to recover ever again. In a nutshell, learning has to be continuous and focused for specialization and growth orientation.

3

LEARN FROM OTHERS' MISTAKES TOO

As I stand at the age of sixty-four years in 2015 with twenty-one different types of successful global assignments, when I hark back to the memory of my childhood, I find it very fresh and green, implying that life is short and time flies. Therefore, it is important to learn more and more in the shortest possible time. Randomly if you decide to learn at an average of one new thing in a day, in one year you learn 365 things. Learn from your mistakes and misadventures but don't leave an opportunity to learn from others' experiences too because in this competitive world, you don't have time to repeat the same mistakes which others have done and learnt from. Study about the reasons of failures of organisations and do your own analysis. Sometimes your in depth analysis will teach you more than what you read because you will see it with the perspective which is more relevant to you.

4

CONTINUOUS LEARNING

The Internet revolution has made the twenty-first century a century with abundant knowledge. With the enormous flow of information in all the fields, you can sometimes get confused and find it difficult to arrive at a correct decision within the available time frame; therefore, it is important to keep yourself updated with continuous training to upgrade you skills. It is more applicable for the persons who are in technical profession. For example, in the software industry you specialise in one version of some package and by the time you could hardly reach to the level of perfection another upgrade is in the market. If you don't move fast you are left behind and your market value goes down. So is the case especially with every technical field. If a surgeon doesn't adapt new procedures which are generally safer and cost effective he loses the patients. Although the non technical fields are also affected by the similar scenario but the pace of changes in them is comparatively slow.

5

NEVER GIVE IN

Everyone wants to be the world's richest person in one's own perspective. Firstly, it is very tough to become the richest person without burning the midnight oil for extended period unless you are born in rich family. But if that be so you still have to have fire in your belly to improve the wealth further or else you lose it. I compare the performance in the profession with a set of marbles rolling down a slope which represents time domain. Each marble represents one important activity in the life. It is your responsibility to keep them above certain target level set by you. They will roll down and you have to prevent them from going down with continuous efforts. The speed of flow can be controlled by the angle of slope you chose. One small distraction will lead to a couple of them slipping your hand and reaching the bottom. If even one marble touches the bottom you get a dent in life in the aspect which that marble represents. It requires your full attention. Similarly, in your life you have to be fully alert with all your senses fully active all the time.

The richness depends on the level of performance where your skills reach a plateau. One of the very commonly narrated stories is that of a beggar lying on the beach. A passer-by asked him, 'You appear to be healthy. Why don't you do some work and earn enough for yourself?' He replied, 'Why should I do anything? I get enough from begging.' The passer-by said, 'If you work harder, you will earn more and more.' To cut the steps of the famous story short, in the last part, the passer-by told the beggar, 'You will be very rich, have plenty of money, and you can spread yourself on the beach and relax.' The beggar replied, 'That's what I am doing now. So why should I make such long and tiring efforts to achieve the same goal?' Well, that's individual attitude. The beggar has his level of contentment. We cannot challenge that.

Another well-known story in Indian medieval history is that of Muhammad Ghauri, who raided Delhi king Prithviraj Chauhan seventeen times and ultimately defeated the Indian king. He got inspiration from ants and succeeded. Ants never leave the load they carry despite it falling any number of times. I have seen their coordination. They can walk forward, backwards and sideways too.

Third is the story of determination I have learnt from small children. I find the good old saying 'Child is the father of man' very true. We all have seen a small child who has just started standing up with support try to climb the bed. He comes crawling, catches the bed sheet on the bed with his very small but strong grip, and then looks around with a smile for appreciation. Then he becomes serious in his second phase of operation, uses both hands, and lifts one leg to climb the bed. Many a time in his first attempt, he fails and falls on his bottoms. When he falls, he looks around and smiles. He again stands up and tries. But if he fails again and again, he gets frustrated and angry over his failures. That is the time he yells with the full force. The mother, who is normally around, comes running and lifts him and makes him seated on the bed. He smiles with a sense of satisfaction and achievement as he has accomplished the mission. Lesson is, if you are failing time and again and you are hell-bent to do the same work, don't waste time; seek the help.

I had brought a similar analogy in my software organization. In development activities especially, sometimes a developer would get stuck on a very simple logic, and the best of struggles wouldn't let him proceed further. My instruction to all the developers was that no one should wait for more than thirty minutes fighting to find the way out but should call immediately for an SOS meeting with relevant colleagues to discuss the problem and find the solution. It used to pay dividends. Advantages were; first, that the developers moved faster; second, they were not stressed; and the biggest was that the team developed interpersonal relations which improved team spirit due to mutual cooperation. Their feelings could not be measured but could be seen and felt with the success of the project.

The overemphasis I am trying to give on this subject is because this is a major problem for many of us who cannot evaluate ourselves about our capabilities, knowledge, financial situations, etc. If you have decided and are hell-bent on making your venture a success, then be patient, have a dogged determination, and learn from not achieving small progresses. Then you are like Abraham Lincoln or are trying to grow a bamboo tree. Out of all the presidents of the USA, Abraham Lincoln had the most turbulent life and delayed success, till he became the president. Undoubtedly, he is the most famous president of the American history. Similarly, you plant a bamboo sapling and keep nurturing it for many years with your untiring efforts, cursing it every day for the poor or slow growth. But after the sixth year or so, generally, it grows at such a pace that all your complaints of slow progress get whipped off.

In short, patience, street smartness, untiring efforts, focused approach, self-confidence to succeed, and determination are the virtues. Sometimes in a tactical decision, losing a battle is very much in order for winning the war.

6

SELF-ESTEEM

I have come across many persons saying that their colleague, senior or junior, has remarked something which has hurt their feelings or prestige. When you deal with human beings, you will likely be exposed to such situation at one time or another. There is no need to react to it as the issue will be aggravated, and you have no time to spend on this non-productive activity. Just ignore, abort, and delete it from your brain. Barking dogs seldom bite. In such situations, remember the poetry of famous poet of undivided India Allama Iqbal:

> Khudi ko kar buland itna, ke har taqdeer se
> pehle, Khuda bande se khud pooche,
> bata teri raza kya hai.

The spirit is this: Elevate your self-esteem so high that even God, before issuing every decree of destiny, should ask you, 'Tell me, what is your intent?'

Meaning, thereby your prestige level should be so high that it cannot be touched by any passer-by.

7

RIGHT THE FIRST TIME

In our profession, we deliver a variety of products to our customers. The product can be in the form of a manufactured item, a study report, a film production, etc. Converting raw material into a final marketable product involves various processes which are the responsibilities of men and machines, including computers. Computers will produce what is programmed for them. Programming is done by *Homo sapiens*; that means any mistake in the process is attributed to the technical skill and state of mind of the programmer. If there is a mistake, the computer will not move forward. The mistakes can be in manual programming. If the workers are alert, they will do a job right the first time (RFT). If they are not in the best of their performance, they will do something wrong, and rework will be required to be done to get the quality-assured output. Rework is frustrating, demotivating, and time-consuming. Since time is money, it is important that the product should be RFT. In a lighter vein, if we imagine a situation where the process is fully automated, we will still need two souls in the work place—one dog to ensure no one touches the machines and another a man to feed the dog.

8

LEADERSHIP

Leadership is the key factor in making a dynamic organizational culture and is the driving force for the success of any organization. A far-sighted, hard-taskmaster, broad-minded, yet humane leader will have no substitute. An organization can have resources of the world, but without smart leadership, nothing proceeds. The performances of organisations mostly depend on the leader. Successful leaders lead by setting personal examples. A 'yes, man' or a shoe shiner boy may reach high in the ladder of promotions but can never be a leader.

Strong leadership attracts the best human resources and extracts the best out of them by retaining them too, while not-so-professional leadership leads to poor morale of the organization, resulting to frequent attrition and low productivity. The thumb rule is that if an employee separates because of any reason, the organization suffers a monetary loss equivalent to the employee's one-year cost to the company.

Now, the question that comes is, where do we get such leaders? Like the promoters the managers at all levels should develop entrepreneurial skills and sense of ownership of the organisation. If we go into the history of India, King Akbar was illiterate and was the only one in the medieval period to be known as Emperor Akbar the Great. In the modern period, known successful business tycoons have been Dhirubhai Ambani, Bill Gates, Steve Jobs, etc.—to name a few of the top-performing first-generation entrepreneurs. None of them has even graduated from any university. Besides these declared billionaires, there are so many merchants churning around the same level or more money quietly sitting in the narrow lanes of wholesale markets in China, Japan, India, Russia etc. Therefore, I am of the opinion that business leaders are born, while CEOs are made in business schools.

9

COMMITMENT

In the present-day world, loyalty and commitment to employers are diminishing. It is due to two way traffic. The employees are looking for higher remunerations and accelerated career while the employer wants to have a more efficient and trimmer organisation with minimum or no dead wood. When it comes to wealth both have reasons to be selfish. This is the modern world, where everything is materialistic. I have come to know that one of the companies in India used to give gold rings to be worn on the ring finger of its employees, meaning that the employees are married to the organization - a lifelong relationship. But what to expect, when the number of divorce cases are also rising?

The efficiency of an employee is the product of motivation and commitment, which can be related like Einstein's formula:

$$E = mc^2, \text{ where, } E \text{ is efficiency, } m \text{ is motivation, and } c \text{ is commitment.}$$

This makes quite sense to me. I recommend that till the time you are serving an organization, don't condemn it. Once you leave the organization, also don't condemn it because you've had a great learning experience either with the dos or don'ts and they have paid you for the duration as per the mutually acceptable terms. So why ridicule any set-up and develop a negative attitude? Attribute it to your learning.

If you are not comfortable with your assignment write down three very good points of the organisation and three very bad points. When you will relook in them, you will have good feeling looking at the good points but for bad points try to analyse that who is responsible for the same and how will you come out of them? You will feel more positive and more at ease.

10

Excellence, Efficiency, and Quality of Output

In all walks of life, whether it is personal or official or domestic, you are judged by the excellence of your conduct in various situations. This behaviour makes you different and a number of shades superior to others. To sum up all the qualities together in one word is attitude. Your *attitude will take you to the altitudes*. Hard work is OK, but more relevant is smart work. You should be able to prioritize your work based on the expected results in the stipulated time. In doing so, you should be able to discriminate between *important* and *urgent*. An activity which is important may not be urgent and vice versa.

Sometimes I like lazy guys—but not who bring shame to organization. They are the ones who will not slog for extended working hours to design a complicated solution to the problems. I strongly believe in the 80:20 ratios in all activities of life. Of problems, 80 per cent have very simple solutions, unless you make them difficult. So give the task to a lazy boy who will bypass the beaten track and come out with a simple, successful solution.

Another guiding principle which I follow is that in my day-to-day performance, I do not try to struggle for *100 per cent quality perfection at the cost of time*. Although the best way is to have 100 per cent quality and 100 per cent punctuality, but if, due to any reasons beyond my control, I am unable to reach that requisite standard; I take the client in confidence and have 100 per cent punctuality and 90 per cent quality of the product with in safe limits.

Quality to my understanding is what customer wants. If you try to give your client coffee in place of tea which he has asked, he will not like it. Although you are offering him more expensive beverage but that is not his choice. Different customers require products of different specifications and standards. If you are a professional who has excellent knowledge and skill, you will deliver the product that meets the desired quality standards of the client. If you achieve it, then the product is most economical because it has been made *right the first time.* Since there is no rework required, *the quality is free.*

11

DECISION-MAKING

Being decisive is a quality of a leader, the accuracy of which comes *only* with experience. Taking no decision is also a decision. I never repent on my past decisions because they were taken in the best interest in accordance with the then existed circumstances. Sometimes, when time is not at the premium, the 'grape wine method' is very useful to feel the pulse of the affected people before implementing a policy decision. This is helpful in fine-tuning the same for faster absorption of everyone in the organization. Correct decisions give you laurels, while a wrong decision gives you experience. You are the beneficiary either way. So why hesitate? Evaluate the situation logically/deliberately, have confidence in you and bash on regardless. Also have a backup plan in critical decisions to guard against the unpleasant reaction of your decision. In the management arena and in personal life, there are no fixed solutions. It all depends on your situation, finances, domestic commitment, and above all, guided by accuracy of your strengths, weaknesses, opportunities, and threats (SWOT) analysis. These parameters vary from person to person based on their situations. When stuck, go on with the SWOT analysis honestly even in your domestic decisions. Write the analysis down on a piece of paper. I have done it successfully many times. But for moving forward, take decisions and do the course correction during the implementation. Sometimes even the best decisions taken may land you in rough weather. I have faced rough weathers too but came out of it with flying colours to share the motivating experiences with professionals and later to tell the stories to my grand children.

> Girte hain sheh-sawar hi maidain-e-jung mein, Woh tifl kya gire, jo ghutno ke bal chalein. (Azeem Dehalvi)

The spirit is this: only a soldier who rides the horse in a battlefield has a chance of falling, but how will those cowards who opt to walk on their knees fall?

Someone may say, 'Is it necessary to fall in the battlefield?' My reply is that whether they win or fall only soldiers get the opportunity to go to battlefield to save their motherland. They never go with an intention to lose the battle. If they are well prepared they win.

12

KNOW YOUR PLATEAU

I compare the life with Marry Go Round in the schools. When it is on move it is difficult to mount on it because other kids will not let you in. So you try once and you are thrown away. After protected attempts you climb on it and go round and round sitting on it till slowly you get up and start enjoying it like others. Isn't it? But if you are scared and don't make attempts, you keep standing out of it.

We all are human beings and have individual personalities. We have our own plans in life and contentment levels. Never keep them fixed and stagnated but keep reviewing them periodically as you proceed ahead in the dynamics of life. The smartness to success is that we are flexible and adaptable to the change of hour and situation. Because of certain pressing circumstances, you may have to mark time at certain levels of success but keep trying for opportunities which will definitely knock on your doors earlier or later for improvement. Or sometimes, even ram at your door. Open the door quickly and jump to grab them tightly. I have experienced this phenomenon which is called, the destiny. The retarding factors in life are temporary. If you are shattered due to certain circumstances, gather your strength step by step and again stand up on your feet like a Bollywood film hero beaten by the villain.

Remember; when you want to ascend, you will find that behind every hill, there is another bigger hill. But there are plateaus too. After reaching a plateau, rest awhile, look around, and search for another hill of challenge. If the attempt is deliberate and accomplished with total determination, success will be on your feet.

13

WORK–LIFE BALANCE

Work, work, work, and no recreation or respite. Many of us feel that if we work for extended hours day in and day out, we are the star performers. Well your boss will always say so. Our brain and body have certain limitations. If we consistently stretch them more than their elastic limits, they stop working. That is probably why the labour law has been made for eight working hours a day. I have observed when people are made to work continuously for more than these working hours, their efficiency drops to 50 per cent. So after eight hours, you get 50 per cent output and you pay double the overtime allowance. Therefore, getting overtime for a protected period is not economical. Yes, randomly, to meet certain targets, there is no harm going on overtime work.

We all have families. When you are not married and are staying with your parents or alone, you come and go any time, and no one objects, except that your mother gets up even in the late hours to serve you hot food when you come home. But when you are married, you have to take out time to be together with your family. Don't forget that this time will never return. So plan your schedule in such a manner that you spend some quality time which is highly recreational with your spouse and children. There is this saying:

> When I was young, I had time
> and energy but no money.
> When I was middle-aged, I had energy
> but no time and money.
> Now I am old, I have time and money but no energy.

If you feel that you are unable to leave the office on time, then either you are inefficient or you waste your time in idle gossips during working hours or you are trying to bite more than what you can chew. Lastly, there is shortage of workforce in your department. For all these you have to take appropriate actions.

Regular exercise not only keeps you physically fit but is also a means of recreation. I've found going for a walk early in the morning as the best physical-fitness activity. It requires only a pair of comfortable shoes. I have gotten solutions to many a problem only during my morning walks.

Never procrastinate in any of the activities, linking one with another. For example: 'I will do this particular thing when this thing will happen.' There is a famous saying that goes like this:

> First, I was *dying* to finish high school and start college, and then I was *dying* to finish college and start working. Then I was *dying* to get married and have family. And then I was *dying* to get my kids settled. I was then too much tired of working and was *dying* to retire and relax. And now I am actually frail, and I am *dying* to *die*. Lastly, when I look back, I realize that time has flown, life has been very short, I had been *dying* only and I've forgotten to *live* the way I wanted.

When you forget to live and realize that you have forgotten, you get frustrated, and your health starts deteriorating faster than normal.

To sum up, we require quality time with family every day, family holiday, some routine physical exercises, recreation and excellent time management.

14

PERSONAL HEALTH AND
TIME MANAGEMENT

The most important aspects of management in life are your health and time management. You are responsible for your good health. Healthy mind in healthy body, is an old saying and true too. You can never get tired doing your work unless your health is bad. Taking healthy food at the right time will keep you mentally and physically alert. You may be undisciplined once in a while but not as a routine. Three main meals and two mid meals will keep you going at a good pace. Many of you are in a chair-bound job; hence, it is all the more important that you have proper exercise depending on your lifestyle. Consult an expert who will advise you about the diet-and-exercise regime based on your lifestyle and body metabolism. I feel too much of both fasting and feasting are harmful to the body.

Being married to your work is as good as marrying a spouse. But to manage your time, like recommended in chapter 13 above, is very important to have a happy, balanced, and tension-free life. Time, if not managed well, is the main cause of stress. There are no rules for time management. Nobody can advise you on this subject because it all depends on your capacity, your working hours, the nature of your work, the travel distance to your workplace, your family life, your hobbies, etc., so make your priorities clear and change them as and when required. Remember this famous quotation:

> You cannot complete the work by sitting extra hours. Work never ends. A hard-working person reaches the plateau faster, while a smart working person keeps ascending. Your family is equally or more important than your client. If your boss stays late, in office every day that is his decision. If you fall in life, neither your boss nor client nor your employer will support you, but your family always will.

Therefore, manage your time well. You should be able to distinguish between *important* and *urgent* work. Urgent works are those which have certain deadlines given by the client or can be a result of your procrastination. These are the tasks which, if not performed within the given time frame, will have immediate adverse effect on your business/performance. Important tasks are the ones which are definitely to be done but can wait for a while because of their long deadline.

15

TURNING AROUND THE ORGANIZATIONS

Upon the completion of my trainings in various technical and managerial fields, it was my turn to be on the top position of small organizations. I was in the army and posted in Bangalore. During one of the dinners hosted by Mr Cool Guy in honour of the visiting Mr Extra-Ambitious, the latter was chatting with me. He asked, 'Are you happy working in the current assignment?' I replied, 'After a number of operational assignments, I was comfortable and was having a bit of peaceful time.' He continued, 'There is an organization under me which is headed by an officer, Mr Very Careless. He is not living up to my expectations. Therefore, I would like to get you transferred to turn around the organization.'

Before I could reply to Mr Extra Ambitious, standing next to me, Mr Cool Guy quickly commented, shaking my hand, 'Congrats, Rajiva, the organization is already in a bad state. You cannot make it worse. Go and take it over the fastest.' That was a very sharp and logical remark. It instantly penetrated my brain. Extra positive and full of confidence to make things happen, I also immediately expressed my interest to take the challenge. In continuation of Mr Cool Guy's remark, I confirmed to Mr Extra-Ambitious my willingness to get transferred to the new station. In one week's time, I received my posting orders to an operation area.

Now the drum was in my neck, and I had no option but to beat it. I had asked for it. It did not take any time for me to do a cursory introspection and decide my course of action. I quickly reached the conclusion that Mr Cool Guy was right; I could not make the organization worse. Instead, with any initiative taken by me in any direction—north, south, east, or west—I will move forward towards improvement. This reminded me of a quotation:

> A bird sitting on a tree is not afraid of the
> branch breaking because her trust is not

on the branch but on her wings. Believe
in yourself.

Trusting myself, I got on to the business. Although the journey was tough (there is an old saying in the army: 'When the going gets tough, the toughs get going.'), I did, not only succeed in bringing this organization operationally fit but also later turned around some other loss-making private companies. I feel:

All problems on this earth have solutions.
Find them. If you don't find them, then
either change the course or learn to live
with them.

As I wrote earlier generally, 80 per cent of problems have very easy solutions and are instantly taken care of, while the balance 20 per cent, though they have solutions, their implementations may take some time, which can be beyond your control.

16

BULLYING THE WEAK PERSON

I have observed that there is a growing tendency in superiors to bully the juniors or weaker people. What is the aim of bullying? To get the job done, in a desirable standard of quality. If the junior colleague doesn't live up to your expectations, should you bully or teach him/her? How do you feel when your boss bullies you? Only a boss bullies, not a leader. I consider a person who bullies as either hollow in skills or not competent to handle the situation.

Bullies generally have very weak personalities. If a junior replies back, he or she immediately becomes apologetic, withdraws in a cocoon, and changes his or her tone. These types of bosses are too scared of their bosses. I have seen their reactions. Juniors are bound to commit mistakes, and leaders are there to clear the mess these youngsters create and teach them. This is learning. If a junior refuses to learn and all your efforts to improve him/her fail, shun him without delay—but don't bully him. Before firing a person, remember that it will cost the business an amount equivalent to his/her one-year cost to the company. Therefore, assess the balance.

Use your smile to change the world.
But don't let the world change your smile.

Always wear a pleasing disposition on your face. It shows how confident, cool, and caring you are. In my life I have never lost temper, but I have raised my voice three times only in forty-two years to wake the sleeping employee up. I believe in the thought that for others' mistakes, why should I burn my blood?

17

Boss Management

Managing a boss is a very deep and vast subject. However, in this introduction, I will touch upon only the most important points. We all are aware of a common saying:

Rule No. 1: The boss is always right.
Rule No. 2: Even if he is not, Rule No. 1 applies.

In all our lives, we have to deal with a variety of bosses. The boss may be a superior executive in the office, your wife at home, sometimes children too, your client, etc. Anybody in your life who has ever been your client is a boss. It depends on the situation. People become bosses for different lengths of time. During the day, your bosses keep changing. Now the problem is how to handle bosses in so many changing situations.

Like any other person, I have also faced this situation nationally and internationally, in the army service and in the private sector in civil service. How to handle situations to see that rule 1 and rule 2 given above apply? The following are a couple of qualities which are required to be inculcated:

(a) Trust your capabilities and self-confidence. Keep sharpening your skills.

(b) Practice diplomatic behaviour. Be polite, nice, and supportive to all but be convinced if something is going wrong.

(c) Always have a cheerful disposition even if you are under pressure. If you cry, 80 per cent of the people will be very happy in their hearts, while the 20 per cent will have no concern. So why cry? But the people in the category of 80 per cent, when they see you cheerful knowing that you are under pressure, they will keep wondering what you are up to.

(d) Be a patient listener and don't follow the example of debates which are more like quarrels taking place every now and then on TV channels.

(e) Never raise your voice during discussions but improve the quality of your argument.

I will sum up all the qualities needed to manage boss in one word: attitude. Believe in this:

Attitude will take you to altitudes.

Some of the traits which are required are the following:

(a) Never bypass or lock horns with your immediate boss or the first reporting manager (FRM). He/she may be tough with all persons reporting to him/her because of the pressure from top to perform. With anything the FRM writes in your appraisal, the reviewing manager, though, has the power to overrule the FRM's remarks but has to justify the action, which I have not seen anybody doing in my forty-one years of service. Even if the FRM gives adverse report, he or she is accountable to the human resource manager, who will ask what actions the FRM has taken well on time to ensure improved performance.

(b) So when you know you have no option but to work under the FRM, then live in win-win situation unless you have some alternatives up your sleeve.

(c) But in doing so, you may not like to follow the path which your FRM asks you to do. Put you point across politely and firmly say, 'Boss, what you are saying is OK, but I would like you to consider my different point of view, which is this.' If he/she insists, 'No, I have considered your point, but still, you do what I say,' then if you are convinced with the logic, follow it like a soldier. There can be a situation when you don't agree with the boss; you may then use your diplomatic communication skill and take it in writing. There can be a situation when you know that the boss avoids giving decisions in writing then, after the discussion, covers it up by e-mail under one pretext or another. Later, if there is a problem, no one can hold you responsible.

18

Backup Plan

We are living in an uncertain world. What happens tomorrow is not known. In this situation, it is important that for all our responsibilities, we should have a big or small backup plan. This plan should be for both your professional life and domestic life. For example, you are working in an organization, and suddenly, you have to leave because of any reason. Do you have enough savings to sustain yourself till you get another assignment, or are your parents rich enough to support you? Tomorrow, there is a medical emergency, and you are not covered by the organization's medical insurance, then how will you cope up with the medical expenses? Irrespective of medical insurance coverage from the employer, I always have one of my own. It is important to cover the period when you are out of job, which may happen any time in life.

I have heard many people say 'Oh, the journey was too long and I got bored' or 'I had to wait for such a long time that it was so boring.' We all have such situations one time or another. I've also had them, but to overcome the boredom, I keep thinking about the backup plans. I make my own situations possible—in the office or at home—and try to find the solution. If you also do the same, you will never be in a dilemma and feel lost when suddenly you are in a thick soup because you have already planned how to swim out. This planning activity gives you self-confidence in your life and you support a cool temperament in the society.

Many a times in our lives, we delegate a job to someone based on our confidence in him/her and the capability of the individual. We also give the target date and time to complete the job. And then at the eleventh hour, when you ask about the result, the output, the individual pulls up a blank face in front of you and says, 'Sir, I got stuck somewhere or another and could not complete the job.' You feel like pulling your hairs and punching him or her on the nose because based on his/her output, you have to build up further. To overcome this phenomenon,

I do two things. One, there is a small display on my table where 'No surprises, please' is written; another one is periodical stage inspections. The result is that all my junior colleagues, whenever they visit my office, will see the display and will get reminded of not giving me a surprise—a psychological warfare—and carrying out the stage inspections will give me confidence that the work in progress is moving in the right direction and pace. So, no tension for me.

PERSONAL
EXPERIENCES

19

LEAD BY EXAMPLE

This incident goes back to the mid seventies. I was the junior-most officer in an organization located in the deep mountains of the Pir Panjal Range in Kashmir. The area that time had a limited number of bridges on the main roads. Other places had causeways or just round stone tracks with river water flowing in them. The stones used to roll off with the force of water very often, causing difficulty in crossing the river. Flash floods could never be predicted in those rivers because the catchment area could be tens of kilometres away.

One day, during the monsoons, it was raining very heavily when someone knocked at my door at around 11 p.m. I opened the door to see a guy standing in front, fully drenched. On my asking if all was well, he replied,

'Sir, the river in our area has suddenly swollen due to flash floods. One of our drivers, Virsa Singh, is stuck with his brand-new 8 ton truck in the river. He is on the driver's seat, with water flowing at his seat level, and refuses to leave the truck.' I could immediately visualize the scene. Virsa Singh was following the customs of the navy. When the ship is sinking, the captain of the ship is supposed to leave last. Virsa Singh was declared as the best driver in the last annual function. He was a very soft-spoken person with exemplary skills in driving in the most inhospitable terrain.

I rang up for the vehicle-recovery crew, and in about twenty minutes, my team was on their way to the river site, about forty kilometres in the mountains. As we were driving up the serpentine curves, I could see there was no respite from the heavy downpour. As we approached the top of the climb to go through the pass, it was pitched dark. An ideal situation to shoot a horror film. I could see lightning in the valley much below us. I had seen lightning above me in the sky but never below me in the valley. Luckily, there were no rivers to cross till the destination.

On reaching the site, I could see in the headlights of the recovery vehicle that the casualty truck was in the river and Virsa Singh was on the driver's seat. The water had receded a lot. I asked my recovery mechanic to anchor the casualty truck firmly. All the crew members were reluctant to do so due to the fear of being swept away with the river flow. The water was about five feet. Without wasting a moment, I pulled out the metallic rope from the winch of the recovery vehicle and dragged it, keeping the towing hook on my shoulder. As I entered the river, all my team members who were scared earlier gathered courage and followed me, and we anchored the truck. Seeing that his casualty truck could not go anywhere, on my persuasion, Virsa Singh also came out of it. We took about two hours pulling the casualty truck safely.

Lesson Learnt: Whenever your team is in crisis, you have to come up and take the lead. The persons under you will feel safe and confident. They will get inspired by your initiative and also automatically bring out their best to assist you. This is the quality of a leader applicable in all walks of life.

20

ACCEPT THE CHALLENGE

After leaving the army on my own will, I worked in a middle-scale telecom-equipment-manufacturing unit. I had reason to be happy and comfortable because the organization was about two kilometres away from my residence, and I didn't have to drive for a protracted time in the heavy traffic of New Delhi to reach my workplace. But it was not to be for a long period. As was written in my fate, I was destined to move from this assignment upon the completion of two years.

Rightly so, I got a call from what is now one of the leading telecom companies. The caller said in a very polished voice, 'I am the HR director calling from XYZ Electronic Push Button Telephones Manufacturing Company. We have shortlisted you for a powwow for a second-level position in our manufacturing organization located in Gurgaon. If you perform as per our expectations, you will be elevated to head the unit in one year.' I accepted the invitation to meet the management. Hearing the place of work as being Gurgaon, which was about forty kilometres from my residence, I was not very keen to take on the assignment, but then I thought that it was only a meeting and there was no harm in it. If nothing else, I would gain some experience. After all they were not magicians that even if I refused to join, they would make me a goat and take me away with them to head one of their units.

Reaching the corporate office, I was guided to a plush conference room which had a touch of styles of international business. The interview panel had three very smartly dressed, seasoned international business persons, including their HR director, on one side and me opposite them. These guys had already done their homework and my background check. I knew about it in advance because the non professional detective who was doing it came and told me about his task. After the usual exchange of pleasantries, without going through any of the so-called interview questions, the director of the company asked me straight, 'Mr Sharma, we have a manufacturing unit located in Gurgaon. We had started this unit seven years ago to cater for the demands of the domestic and international markets. Our best efforts have not till now proved good enough, and alas, we are booking losses year after year. Can you turn this company around the soonest?' It was a bolt out of the blue for me. I replied, 'Can I see the place and working of the unit to quickly assess the situation and give you the answer?' I was trying to buy time. With my experience, I have a knack of observing things fast supported by my trust on intuition. I also believe in feel-good factor on first look. The director was probably in too much of a hurry to listen 'Yes' from me; otherwise, he was not interested in talking further. He asked me, 'Say yes or no.' Within a fraction of a second, I recalled the comment of Mr Cool Guy at Bangalore. I told myself, *Come on. Damn it. The unit is already in a bad state, and I cannot make it worse. Any step for improvement in any direction will add a feather in my cap.* I replied with full confidence, 'Yes, I will turn the loss-making company around.' To my surprise, they asked me to wait, and in half an hour, I was given an offer with more than double the then my cost to company perks. Above the fatter remuneration, I was going to head the organization and the challenge to turn the company around soon. I was very excited with the challenge and started itching to break the ice.

Monitoring my way of working and my capability of pulling the elephant holding its tail through a pinhole and becoming optimistic on foreseeing the vegetation in the barren land, the management not only made me the top person in three months against the earlier plan of one year of my joining but also challenged me to compete for Golden Peacock National Quality Award 1997, which my organization won leaving behind eighty-four competitors. I also successfully turned the company around in total fourteen months. How I met the challenge is a long story. In my university days I have been playing contract bridge tournaments. I play by Ely Culbertson's method and believe that:

> It is not necessary that every time you get a strong hand or a weak hand, the smart players, with the help of his or her partner, make the moves so sharp that even with their weak hand, the opponents collapse like a house of cards. All depends on your accurate assessment and capability of handling the situations with finesse.

Lesson Learnt: Life is full of risks. Take the challenge of life with a positive mindset. Have faith in your approach and skills. If you are confident, you don't feel you are gambling. Keep moving forward step by step in the same way as you climb a mountain, but logically and deliberately, with firm feet on ground. You will definitely succeed. Climbing may be tough, but the view from the top of the peak is very soothing, refreshing, and gives you a terrific sense of achievement. The feeling is out of this world and highly motivating for bigger achievements.

21

WELFARE OF WORKERS FIRST

I had newly joined a private organization responsible for the manufacturing of electronics equipment. In line with my way of working, I had generally put a number of activities in place, but there were some small things which could not apparently be seen on the surface. The salary day used to be the last working day of the month. That meant the head of the organization used to sign the salary sheet on the second to the last working day, in the morning, and the same would be sent to the bank so that the amount would be available for the employees on the last working day. The managers were given the salary cheques on the second to the last working day in the same analogy. The finance manager, in his briefing, had informed me of this procedure.

It was my first month in the organization. The month was July. Therefore, logically, I should have signed all the cheques and salary sheet for remittances on 30 July in the morning. But I was surprised when the finance manager came to my office on 28 July with only one cheque drawn in his name for his salary for my signature. I asked him, 'Today is not the salary documents signing day. How comes you have come yourself for your cheque only?' He replied, 'I am the finance manager. I always take my cheque first. This has been the system in the organization.' I found it difficult to control my disapproval with sarcasm, but somehow, I did so and replied in a polite but firm tone, 'I overrule the old tradition. Henceforth, my first signatures will be on the salary sheet of supervisors and workers, second will be on the cheques of managers, in which your cheque will be in the end, and last will be mine.' This was in line with a powerful teaching that the army officers uphold the highest, the moral and ethical values inscribed in the oak panelling at the entrance of Chetwode Hall in Indian Military Academy, Dehra Dun. It goes like the following:

> The safety, honour, and welfare of your country come first, always and every time. The honour, welfare, and comfort

of the men you command come next.
Your own ease, comfort, and safety come
last, always and every time.

In the private sector, I also strictly follow this teaching. The only modification I've done has been that in the first line, I've replaced *country* with the name of the organization. And with this approach I have been successful.

Lesson Learnt: Look after the welfare of your team, and they will return the same in the form of improved productivity.

22

WORK CULTURE: EXTRA-TIME WORK

In my work life, I have heard people say that one particular person is very hard-working. He keeps working till the late hours. I hate this culture from the core depth of my heart and mind. I consider this culture attributed to either the person being not adequately equipped with relevant skills and experience or wasting his/her and his/her colleagues' time with gossiping around.

When I joined this new company, I observed that the production line used to close down at 5.30 p.m., while the heads of the department (HoD) used to leave the office after three hours. The reason was that the then unit head also used to leave at around the same time. Still not taking over as head, one day, I peeped into the boss's room, thinking that he must be on his desk, planning something great. I noticed for the next five minutes he was holding one component-mounted printed circuit board in his hand, leaning back in his chair with his eyes closed. First, I thought he was deep in his thoughts, but since I had also worked in R & D of the coveted Bharat Electronics Ltd., Bangalore, in the design team of the fire-control radar, I concluded that the boss was sleeping. It was his routine. When I took over the unit, first order which I gave to the HoDs was that everyone should be in the workplace by 8.50 a.m. and see the workers ushering in. From 9.00 a.m. to 9.30 a.m., everyone would do his or her personal job, like payment of personal bills and school fees, booking the domestic gas, etc. From 9.30 a.m. to 10 a.m., they would collect the production data and come to the 10 a.m. daily production-review meeting headed by me. Later in the evening, when workers leave by 5.30 p.m., the HoDs would leave before 6.30 p.m. Anybody staying after that time in the office as a routine had to explain to me the reason. It worked very well. I could feel the change in the air. The staff appeared happier and more efficient. They had some quality time to spend with their near and dear ones. Sounds simple, but this had a very big impact to improve the work culture.

Lesson Learnt: We are all human beings. We need a social life too. Our families want to spend some quality time with us. They need to be appreciated, loved, and given attention. After all, we only work to look after them.

23

COURAGE OF CONVICTION

All employers want to grow multi fold in the minimum possible time and cost. In achieving the same, they tend to commit more than their capacity. And when they are unable to meet the customers' target, they have to cut a sorry figure. I've never committed more production output than my very well and realistically calculated capacity and resources. The resources can only be stretched up to their elastic limits. A situation came that the management wanted to offload to me, some additional production from another plant which had some problems. They wanted me to make 50,000 extra number of equipment over and above we were producing to cover the shortfall of another sister unit. The raw material held in our works in the store was that for only

35,000. At the end of the financial year, no supplier was ready to provide raw material for another 15,000 number of units at very short notice. I told the management that it was not possible for me to cover the shortfall. The management took it with a pinch of salt, but I was happy that I didn't keep anybody in the dark. It was different that I produced 15,000 equipment in the next month which was counted against next month's production.

Lesson Learnt: Never keep your bosses in the dark and refrain from giving them shocking surprises. Have courage to stand up and say what is realistic and what is not. We are neither magicians nor super humans. Don't kill yourself and your team by chasing impossible and unrealistic targets.

24

SWOT Analysis

We all have learnt strength, weakness, opportunities, and threats analysis (SWOT) during our academic courses, and many of us have used it also, whenever needed. I am in very strong favour of this analysis in all walks of life. I have used it very effectively in decision-making at my workplace and at home. Also, I strongly recommend using the same whenever someone gets stuck. If you are in a dilemma, just don't waste your time; get on to SWOT. Do it unbiased and honestly on a paper.

While heading the works in Goa in the late nineties, one day I found my secretary sitting in a very gloomy posture. When I asked her the reason for the different disposition unlike her usual one, instead of answering, she started crying. Sensing that there was something deeper than what it appeared, I got her a cup of coffee to put her at ease and then asked again. She replied, 'I have been separated from my husband for four years. He left me when I was carrying my son and never even came to look me up in hospital when I delivered. I have never even seen him or met him since we separated. Now, tomorrow is the final decision in the court for the divorce.' I told her, 'If he has not cared even to see his own son and never bothered about you both, then why should you have any anxiety about the divorce? You should rather be happy that you are getting rid of him and you are going to be free bird.' I continued, 'OK, do the SWOT analysis of this situation. The problem is that you are going to have divorce tomorrow.' She calmed down and appeared more confident, probably hoping to find herself in a better state of mind in the court.

Next day, she came to the office after hearing the judgement on the divorce petition with an ear-to-ear smile and almost danced in the aisle of the office. She came straight to my office and said, 'Thank you, sir. I got the divorce, and I am very happy.' I asked, 'How come twenty-four hours back, you were very sad and nervous, and now you are so jubilant?' She responded, 'All credit goes to my SWOT analysis.' She had done the SWOT analysis and reached the conclusion that it was in her and her son's best interest that the divorce should go through.

Lesson Learnt: When stuck in decision-making in any situation, the SWOT analysis will bail you out.

25

BETWEEN THE DEVIL AND THE DEEP BLUE SEA

On completion of a successful financial year at the end of March, I had asked the management for some rest-and-recuperation break in the first week of April. Since I had the reputation—which was true too—of not taking many leaves, it was approved without any preconditions. We as family decided to go to Dehra Dun and move around, keeping it as a firm base. The plan was to have a full week out. Only in the midweek did I receive a call from the executive assistant that the managing director (MD) would like to meet me as soon as I returned. I fixed up the meeting and went to call on him on the instant Monday.

After exchanging pleasantries, the MD asked me if I was interested in going to Goa to head another work of the same enterprise. The Goa work was not producing any electronics product. They were in for the manufacturing of high-density polyethylene (HDPE) ducts in collaboration with an American company. I knew the product and also the location of the plant. Earlier also, there was a vacancy for head of works, but my expression of interest to join the same was turned down by the management on the pretext that the product was mechanical engineering based. On hearing the offer, I was not surprised because in any organization, you are given opportunities based on their convenience. Your experience, learning, and specialization don't matter.

With that background, I asked the MD, 'Earlier, you turned my request down on the pretext that I am not a mechanical engineer.' Since the bucking had to end with him, he answered, 'We already have a mechanical engineer as head of department [production]. You only have to manage the managers.' I was, in any case, looking for a change because after turning the company around, taking them out clear from tax disputes, and getting the organization a national award, there was no challenge left for me. Everything was on auto mode, and I was standing on a plateau. The MD further told me that the work at Goa had not been making any profit for over two years. Target was to turn the organization around. As usual, I took the challenge because *I couldn't have made it worse.*

I accepted the offer, but then he asked, 'What will happen to your son's education? He has just cleared eleventh standard and moved to twelfth, which is an education board examination. Would he be able to handle the midsession changes?' I replied, 'If he will study, he will do well anywhere.' On hearing my decision to take my son in midsession to Goa from Noida, there were many unwanted advises that started coming forth from my peers. Ignoring all of them, we shifted to Goa lock, stock, and barrel. How I handled this challenge of my son's education successfully is a different story. However, the end result was that with arts subjects, he got four distinctions out of five subjects. We were happy with the result of our bold decisions. I am not shaky in taking decisions because I already plan a back up strategy to cover up the failures.

On arrival at the work, I examined the state of morale of the workers, which, I found, was satisfactory. The availability of material was OK. There was some problem with state electricity power connection, which I resolved within one week after meeting the chief minister of Goa personally.

The basic problem which surfaced out was that of non-availability of market. In order to keep the workers busy, the raw material was converted to the finished product with the hopes of receiving an order from a state PSU that had shown interest in our ducts and had purchased some for one of the expressways. Thus, the excise bonded warehouse was full of finished products. I did my calculations and found that the inventory-carrying cost was a major contributor to the red bottom line in the balance sheet of the company. I asked the director of this business, 'How long can we wait for the purchase order? Non-moving inventory was one of the big reasons of loss.' He informed me that the customer's name had been printed on the duct, and it was not sure if they were going to buy it in the near future. With the laying of optical fibre cable to replace the copper cables still in the infancy stage, there were hardly any buyers elsewhere. I told him, if the ducts were buried underground, no one would see the name of the customer printed. But he had strong reservations and didn't agree with me. Incidentally, the HDPE ducts are first buried in the underground network with a manhole cum junction box located at an average length of one kilometre. The optical fibre cables were blown in these ducts with the help of a blowing machine from junction box to junction box.

Finding it not a very difficult situation to solve, I presented two plans to liquidate the sleeping inventory—first, that we find a customer who wouldn't care for someone else's name printed on the ducts, and second was to shred the ducts. The first action wouldn't have led to any loss, while shredding would have cost us initial manufacturing and then reprocessing expenditure. Now, who would take the decision? My director was very shaky and postponed the decision until the quarterly performance review meeting (QPRM) scheduled for the next week.

The MD flew in for QPRM. I had planned a factory visit for the MD and the director before going in for the formalities of QPRM. My director had done the financial calculations for the loss which would have incurred if the shredding was done. I had my calculations, which were different from the boss's arithmetic and not acceptable to him. The difference was that I insisted on including the cost of initial manufacturing as loss. But maybe out of extra zeal, he got the ducts manufactured and was unable to sell them and was thus not ready to take the dent in his calculations.

We were standing in the bonded warehouse. As expected, the MD asked me what could be done with the finished product stacked there. Before I could answer, the director replied, 'We will shred the complete stuff and wait for the purchase order before remanufacturing the same.' An obvious question was about the financial aspect. The director enthusiastically showed his calculations to the MD, who turned to me and asked, 'Do you agree with the calculations?' I put across my point that the loss would be more than what the director was showing because he had not taken into account the cost of initial manufacturing. The MD agreed with me and asked how I was going to proceed. I said, 'I will try to sell maximum product as it is, and if something is left, as a last resort, I will shred the balance but will include the initial manufacturing cost in the cost of remanufacturing calculations.' The MD saw the sense in it and told me to go ahead. The director gave me a growling look and protested the decision unsuccessfully.

My position was that of between the devil and the deep blue sea. I decided to go ahead selling the ducts the soonest. It was in the best interest of the organization. I called up one of our bulk customers. I explained the situation to him. He was in urgent need of 102 kilometres of ducts. I jumped from my chair. As luck would have it, I had exactly the same length to sell. In one hour of my call to the customer, I got the purchase order through fax with the dispatch details. I was very happy. I immediately called my manager (logistics) and told him to dispatch the complete stuff before the close of business (COB) that day.

We needed seventeen trucks. We had an annual contract for supply of trucks with a famous NCR-based company with HQ at Gurgaon. Their regional manager, when asked to provide seventeen trucks at a very short notice, showed the inability to produce the same. Without waiting even a moment, I called up the owner of a transport company located in Gurgaon who in turn mobilized the trucks from the nearby locations in states of Maharashtra and Karnataka. The trucks started making a beeline on the entrance gate. Loading, billing, and excise clearance were done as parallel activities. The mission of dispatching the complete ducts from the warehouse was accomplished before COB.

I had arranged a formal dinner for the visiting MD and the director at Hotel Cidade De Goa. I reached the venue earlier to receive the MD and the director. Immediately upon entering the banquet hall, the MD asked me, 'So what is the decision taken? Could you find a customer?' I took a sigh and replied, 'One hundred and two kilometres of duct loaded in seventeen trucks would have crossed the Goa State boundary by now on their way to Madhya Pradesh.' Naturally, he was happy and I was very satisfied, but the director was visibly very uncomfortable. Following day, I showed them the empty warehouse.

This was the beginning of my cold war with the director, which later led to my separation from the company, and turned out to be a blessing in disguise. I got a very high-paying and prestigious international assignment in the United Nations in International Civil Services.

Lesson Learnt: Learn to accept the challenges and take calculated risks. Once plunged into action, be positive, show determination, and make things happen. Also, try to avoid confrontation with the boss, but if you are left with Hobson's choice, then catch the bull by its horns and move ahead. If you are clean, honest, and logical in approach, your trouble will be short-lived, and very soon you will make up for the loss. I did so.

I remember a *doha* (two-line poetry) of the poet Kabir:

> Jin khoja tin paiyan, gahare pani painth.
> Main bora duban dara, raha kinare baith.

Meaning, thereby, whoever searched and made an attempt, sitting in the deep water (concentrating in risky conditions), achieved whatever was desired. I was scared of sinking and thus kept on sitting on the bank.

26

CAUSE-EFFECT STUDY TO SOLVE PROBLEMS

In the mid seventies, I was posted in an equipment-repair workshop located on the western part of Jammu and Kashmir. We were part of Border Roads Organization (BRO) under the Ministry of Shipping and Transport. Our responsibility was to maintain all equipments in the particular sector up to the second echelon of repairs.

The organization had the personnel mixed from BRO and army. Since both the personnel were from different organizations, they used to wear different uniforms. For BRO, it was khaki colour, while for the army, it was olive green. The army personnel were happy to work with BRO because of a lesser degree of regimentation, but on the other hand, BRO personnel were not satisfied with the lower remunerations and less perks compared to their army counterparts. After around twenty-five years of inceptions of BRO and living in disparity along with army personnel, a wave to seek matching compensation had started among the ranks and files of BRO workers. Although in the core depth of their hearts, the army leaders were in favour of the demands, but getting a proposal made and taking the same through the bureaucratic channels for implementation was a herculean and slow task.

Monitoring the developments of growing unrest, news came from the eastern sector that the personnel of two big BRO establishments located in Tezpur had gone on strike, which had been smartly handled. The names of the persons that spearheaded the strike were also circulated to us.

One day, when I went to my office in the morning, the supervisor in charge of administration came to me to inform me that one of the strike leaders from Tezpur had been posted to our unit and he had already reported on duty. As per the procedure, the new arrivals were brought to the office of head of the unit by the supervisor in charge of administration along with their personal documents to the head of the unit. It is formal affair, I told the supervisor for arranging his meeting with the head of the unit.

Meanwhile, I went on my routine round of the workshop to take first-hand information of the activities on the ground. I knew all the personnel working with me by face and name. As soon as I started my round, I saw a strange face on the shop floor. At the first look, I noticed the rebellious appearance. He had uncombed hair longer than expected, his beard was not shaven for three or four days, and he gave him an angry look. I approached him and asked, 'Are you Darshan Kumar from Tezpur?' He confirmed with minimum words. My second question was 'Why have you not taken a haircut and shaved?' He replied, 'There are no barbers authorized in the organization.' I was not surprised with the answer from a union leader. Keeping my cool, I asked him, 'Even washer man is not authorized. Therefore, Darshan, you will not wash your clothes?' He had no answer. The supervisors informed me that Darshan had been an ace mechanic but had been a victim of poor processing of his financial claims.

Knowing fully well the problem, I asked the supervisor to call Darshan to my office. After hearing his part of grievances, I was convinced that anybody in his position would behave the way he was and look hopeless. His authorized financial claims were pending for flimsy reasons. *Lack of money is the root of all evils.* And in his case, he was deprived of his authorization. I was sympathetic to him and assured him of fastest settlement. He challenged me, 'Sir, you are a junior officer only, and many senior-level officers have not been able to provide me the relief.' Normally while in uniform, such comments were not taken kindly. But I knew that his problem was genuine and he was really suffering. I assured him that I would do my best, and that should be good enough.

I immediately called my chief clerk and gave him my action plan to be implemented on white-hot priority. He proceeded, and within one month, the first financial claim was passed and paid. Seeing other claims being processed aggressively, Darshan became my confident ace mechanic. It took about four months till he got all the pending claims. He was a changed person altogether. Very enthusiastic, positive in attitude, loyal, yet very helpful, to the clients. These were the original sleeping qualities in him which I took out. He started looking well groomed and full of energy. On doing the analysis of his claims problems, I found that there were no serious hurdles, but the concern clerks were not addressing the problems systematically. When we focused on to them, solutions started flowing.

Although he was comfortable, sometimes he was instigated by his peers about the disparity in the service conditions. At my level, I was unable to do anything. So I decided to give him importance and also detached him from such instigators. I placed Darshan at a remote site where communication with HQ was only by first, walking twenty kilometres on foot and then forty kilometres by road transport, crossing three rivers. Before posting him there, I told him the truth, 'Darshan, I am sending you to milestone 20 to independently take care of the maintenance of machines deployed. You are my trusted person; I don't have to worry about the uptime of the equipment.' Since it was a challenge and he was made directly responsible for the working of a small detachment as the head, he felt elated and accepted to move to the new location. Believe me; I never had any problems of any type from him. I used to visit him once a month.

Everyone was very satisfied with his work. Although he never gave me any problem after that, I used to feel guilty that he was being roughed out in a remote area. When I used to think how I could help him more than what was in my powers, I couldn't see anything in the horizon. At times I used to get restless on this account.

At last, the day came when the waiting was over. I got a letter from the directorate general of Border Roads, seeking nominations for engineering equipment mechanics for deputation to Indian Road Construction Corporation, Iraq. I hurriedly flipped the pages to the one where the qualitative requirements for the position were written. To my pleasure, I found Darshan matched each and every one of them. I made a very strong proposal, recommending him to go on deputation to Iraq. He was selected, and we dispatched him to a foreign posting with comparatively much higher remunerations and thus higher saving potential. I took a sigh of relief. I was so satisfied that I could help make a person who had diverted to a wrong path return to the mainstream.

Lesson Learnt: God has made all persons equal. The circumstances make them good or bad. To resolve the problem, go to the deep, into the root cause, and have patience without losing temper. The affected person at grass-roots level will give you the true picture.

27

RESPONSIBILITY
RESTRICTS THINKING

I was running a software business dealing with development on Microsoft technology, .net, C, C++, etc. during the daytime and providing after-hour support to the tailor-made programs for monitoring the training of mentally challenged students based in Ohio, USA. Naturally, as the top person of the organization in India, I was responsible in ensuring performance for both the pillars of the company. Truly speaking, it was too much work. The development was done in the daytime in Delhi while the customer support was provided from Gurgaon at night.

I was aging and residing in Noida. It was strenuous to personally visit both places very often. I had been managing it well but at a cost. Looking for an opportunity to bail out of this hectic schedule, I had been in continuous touch with the HR department of United Nations for a suitable slot. At last, I got one for a peacekeeping mission in Darfur. (The governorate of Darfur is located on the western border of Sudan, touching Chad in Africa.) I was told to report to the UN Logistic Base in Italy and, after two weeks of training/briefing, to proceed to Darfur.

It was a good opportunity, so I handed over my software activities to one of the senior officers who was about to retire from the service and proceeded to join the UN assignment. After briefing in Italy, I landed at Khartoum airport in Sudan. It was a thermal and cultural shock too. After certain mandatory induction formalities, I was booked in a UN air shuttle service from Khartoum to the city of El Fasher. The flight was for about ninety minutes over the desert—yes, an absolute desert.

On landing at the destination, the facility manager at the reception told me that he was giving me the best guest house in the mission. I was happy. But when I reached the guest house, I found that it was a proper house with four bedrooms. Depending on the size, the rooms were shared by two or more residents. I had never lived in a shared accommodation even in my university hostel. Since it was the best accommodation, I had no option but to occupy a bed. This guest house had a common dinning place in the lobby, a common laundry, a kitchen, and washrooms—all located outside the main building.

I started cooking my own food as the one which was available in the official cafeteria was not suiting my system and my timings. During the course of cooking, I met a co resident; He was an interesting person and weighed 350 pounds. He started coming and watching me cook. I used to invite him to share the meal, which he used to accept, as he could not cook and also was getting fed up with the meals from the cafeteria. This became a routine for dinner. One day, he told me, 'You cook and I wash the utensils.' I agreed, and this arrangement worked well. On one of the holidays, he said that he was going to purchase grocery and I shouldn't do that in that week. I agreed because the load should not be on one person. In the evening, when he returned, I asked him, 'Gerry, what have you bought? Let me go for cooking.' He replied, 'Chief, I have bought a good liquid soap and some scrubbers.' I said, 'That's very fine. This is the material required for your part of activities, but how about grocery?' He gave me a lame look and said that he couldn't decide what to buy so he purchased the cleaning material and came. I couldn't step out to pick up some items for cooking as the curfew used to be imposed from 6 p.m. till 6 a.m. the next day. There was no problem because we consumed the emergency rations. I was not disturbed because generally, people think only in line with what they do and the environment where they live.

Lesson Learnt: Delegate the responsibility in accordance to the type of duties the workers are performing. For any deviation, explain the changed requirement thoroughly and cross-check for correct understanding; otherwise, one gets surprised, as I got.

28

LIAISON WITH ANYONE PAYS

While I was still in the process of settling down and starting to open my wings in El Fasher, Darfur, one day at 10 p.m., I got a mail from the top person in the mission, asking my expression of interest for going to Addis Ababa, Ethiopia, to establish an office of our mission. Following my guiding principle, 'I cannot make it worse.' I accepted yet another challenge and confirmed my willingness. Next morning, when I reached the office, the atmosphere was hot. I was called for initial briefing. The detailed one was scheduled for the next day. The time of the meeting was not decided. The next day I reached the office and was told to make my travel arrangements on a date and reach the conference room for a detailed discussion immediately.

Priority for both the jobs was *important* and *urgent*. I decided to go to the travel office first and gave them the travel details and then proceeded for the briefing. Here I could have done the other way around, but I thought that the travel office would start working as soon as they got the details and they would have some input for me when I returned from the briefing. I was right; when I returned after two hours, I had my air tickets ready. Booking was *urgent*, while attending the briefing was *important*.

I got settled down very fast in Addis Ababa, and due to the nature of my work, I had to develop good relations with all the concerned authorities the fastest. I was fully functional in about ten days in the new office.

Sundays used to be weekly holidays in Ethiopia, while in Sudan, Friday was the holiday. On one of the Sundays, I was having problems with internet in my hotel, so I decided to go to the office and check the mails. The chief of my peacekeeping mission, the special representative of the secretary general of the UN (SRSG), who was in Addis Ababa to attend the African Union summit, called me at 11 a.m. and told me that he wanted his official Lear jet at the Addis Ababa airport by 4 p.m. the same day as he wanted to reach Khartoum by 5.30 p.m. to attend a very urgent talk between the government and a tribal chief. If he did not reach to attend the meeting, there could be an armed conflict between the two, leading to bloodshed.

The concern for me was to be an instrument in avoiding the bloodshed, and the challenge was to arrange the aircraft. The process was to ask permission from the Ministry of External Affairs, Sudan, to let the aircraft exit the country and permission from the Ministry of External Affairs, Ethiopia, to let the aircraft enter and then leave again for Sudan. With it being Sunday, Sudan was working, while Ethiopia had a weekly holiday.

I had developed a good liaison and a friendly relationship with the MEA, resulting to getting all permissions within two hours. The Lear jet took off from El Fasher and reached Addis Ababa on time. The SRSG flew to Khartoum on time, and conflict was avoided.

Lesson Learnt: We should be able to prioritize the work based on urgency and importance. Secondly, wherever we are, we should first develop cordial working relationship with the people who have authorities and could be helpful in our day-to-day life.

29

BE HUMANE AND COMPASSIONATE

After turning around two profit centres in India, I thought whatever I had to learn from the organizations I had done or had to implement. There was nothing exciting for me in the near future till the transformation matured. So I decided to resign before I could even get an alternative assignment. I was confident that something would definitely fall in the front.

I was browsing the Internet, looking for some challenging opportunity, late in the night; I got hooked on to the UN job site. I was surprised. I got a vacancy announcement (VA) suiting exactly my profile. UN was all new to me—the system and the organization. But to me, going to unexplored places had been thrilling. I applied for the vacancy. One week later, while I was at my computer at around 11 p.m., I got a phone call. The caller said, 'I am speaking from UN HQ, New York. You have applied for a position in peacekeeping mission in Iraq. We have found you suitable for the job. Are you still interested?' Shocked by such quick response, I didn't know what to say. However, I didn't want to play a blind hand thus asked the caller, 'What are the terms and conditions, place of posting, and above all, the remunerations?' On hearing that the assignment was in war-torn Iraq, place of posting was in Baghdad City, and remunerations were parallel to the salary structure in Washington DC and fully income tax free in US dollars, I expressed my interest on the telephone, followed by a signed scanned copy through the computer, and lastly, first thing in the morning, by sending an ink-signed copy by the DHL courier. How I reached Iraq after this acceptance is a long story full of hurdles, but I succeeded.

I reported my arrival in the Baghdad office, and an introduction meeting was arranged with the head (SRSG) of the UN mission for assigning me the position. He welcomed me to the mission and expressed his concern that I might not find the job stimulating as I had been actively involved in giving results in profit-oriented companies. Honestly, I thought, *with those types of perks and salaries, I could do anything under any trying conditions.* SRSG decided to appoint me in the health sector. I questioned him, 'I am a telecom engineer. What would I do in the health sector?' He replied, 'You are an international civil servant. You can be placed anywhere. We don't have telecom sector. You join the health sector and start planning to establish the same. Once it is done, you head the telecom sector.' Wow, it was another new challenge for me, and I was thrilled. I was supposed to observe the sourcing and distribution of medicines in the country so that the chemicals and salts banned by the security council of the UN were not smuggled in Iraq as medicines, and used for making weapons of mass destructions, which was not authorized.

My first observation assignment started, and I was supposed to go to a town called Tikrit in Iraq. I had an English-speaking driver who was my interpreter for Arabic too and also a representative of the Ministry of Health, government of Iraq. He was a health professional and was assigned to facilitate the observations on the ground. As scheduled, I reached the primary health centre (PHC) and went to the director's office to start my work. All the Iraqis had been very courteous to me.

They had special respect for Indians for various historical reasons.

When I came out of the office, I found around 50 women clad in black *burkas* (veils) standing around my Land Cruiser. The director of the facility told me that they were waiting for me. New to the system, I didn't know UN norms to handle such delegations. On asking the reason of their gathering, they told me that all of them were pregnant and had not been given even one shot of mandatory anti-tetanus injection. The reason was that the drug was put under embargo by the sanctions put on Iraq. I was shocked. It sent shivers down my spine. This I thought was an inhuman restriction. I assured them of the best of my efforts to get the embargo lifted and the serum released.

The first thing I did after reaching the mission HQ was to make a strong case based on humanitarian needs and forwarded it to the authorities in the UN HQ for releasing the anti-tetanus injections on humanitarian grounds forthwith. Faster than expected, I got the release order. I jumped with joy. The pleasure of my success was so much that I got the dispatch of ampoules to the correct destinations expedited on priority. I informed the director of the primary health centre about my success and also the date of my next visit to him for releasing the same. I was itching and getting restless to go to the PHC, but I was bound by the security restrictions for movement.

Anyway, the day came when I reached the PHC to release the anti-tetanus vaccines in enough quantity to the facility. When my vehicle entered the premises, I could see a crowd of burka-clad (veil) women again in the veranda. The director told me that those were the same women who had earlier met me and had asked for the vaccine. He had informed them that the vaccine had arrived and would be released on that day. Upon seeing me, they started saying something simultaneously in Arabic. From their gesture I could make out that they were thanking me. Many of them had brought self-baked cakes too to express their happiness and gratitude. I still get goose pimples in my body when I think of this incident. I got immense job satisfaction.

Lesson Learnt: To resolve a human problem, a systematic and compassionate approach assessing through the humanitarian angle should be taken. Success leads to you getting a tremendous sense of satisfaction.

30

CALCULATED RISKS

Once, I was posted in a place called Rajouri located deep into the mountains in the northern part of India. It was in the centre of my area of operation, which was spread up to ninety kilometres in all directions by the road. Since the roads were either maintained or made new, a variety of road-construction equipment were deployed all around. Going to ascertain the operational reliability of these was part of my routine activity. Some equipment were located in places with no communication links. My wife used to stay in Rajouri, in our officers' Mess, along with our two years old daughter. One day, I had to go to Poonch, a town about eighty kilometres away in the mountains. When I was on my way back, I hit a roadblock. It was a landslide-prone area, and big boulders had started rolling down along with the loose soil. I had told my wife that I would return by late evening. I had two choices—one, that I stay back and start again once the slide was over, but it was not possible to calculate when it would stop and start again, or second, to quickly evaluate the time the boulders would roll from the top to the road and the time required by me to run through the damaged road. I wanted to reach Rajouri the same day. I told my driver to stop the Jeep and did my calculations. When I found that it could be a risk but balance was tilting towards the safe side, I told my driver to run through the slide. He was a bit shaky and gave me a hesitant grin. I took over the steering wheel, put the vehicle in four-wheel-drive high, and told the driver to hold himself cautiously on his seat and keep looking at the top of the mountain to caution me. I drove through the patch at the maximum speed possible and came out safe. The driver was sweating. I looked at him and laughed aloud like a successful warrior. He asked me to stop for a while till his breathing came back to normal.

When I look back now, I sometimes feel that what I did was a risky decision, but then I reconcile with the thought that I was twenty-seven years old and was full of adventurous spirit. Maybe sitting now at sixty-four years in 2015, I would be reluctant to do action replay.

Lesson Learnt: Learn to take risks—calculated ones, not foolhardy ones. Risk-taking capabilities vary from person to person and situation to situation. There is no thumb rule for this. Your risk calculation should include the alternate plan also in case you fail. Your success depends on your experience and self-confidence.

31

TAKE SECOND OPINION IN CASE OF HEALTH

When I started a software company, I had many challenges. One of them was to recruit the staff members who were qualified and had relevant experience. Being from an army background, I was concerned about their medical fitness also. This information used to help me in the distribution of work and tasking, considering the limitations of the individuals.

In accordance with this approach, during the recruiting process, I asked one young lady software testing-engineer, 'Do you have any medical problem which you feel could be a limiting factor in discharging your duties?' She replied, 'Generally, everything is OK, except that one doctor has told me that my heart is weak and I will die within the next ten years.' I was not shocked by this statement when she told me the name of the hospital where she had gone. I asked her another question, 'When did he tell you this? And did you feel any problem in your day-to-day life?' She said, 'Two years back, during my first childbirth. And I am doing perfectly fine in my routine life.' I recommended for her to go for a thorough check-up in one of the leading super speciality heart hospital located at a walking distance from our office. She took the appointment and went for the consultation as scheduled. Before going to the hospital, she called me on phone and said, 'Sir, on your recommendation, I am going to the hospital, but I am scared. What will happen if this hospital confirms what the other has diagnosed? Please pray for me.' I built up her confidence and encouraged her. She went. With my general experience, she never sounded like a person with a heart ailment. At around 3 p.m. the same day, I got the call from her. 'Sir, my proper heart check-up has been done. And the super specialist has certified that I am perfectly fine for my age. There is no ten-year limit for my life.' She disconnected the phone, and within five minutes, she was in my office, unable to stop grinning with an ear-to-ear smile.

Now in 2015, more than ten years have passed without any problems. She is a mother of two babies, all in excellent health.

Lesson Learnt: Sometimes, we start believing in wrong advises without having a second opinion and start destroying our today with deteriorating performance. Whenever in such situation, always ask for second opinion.

CONCLUSION

I have put my real-life experiences in a simple language and avoided making it a heavy reading. I have experienced that not hard work but a balanced, smart work helps you succeed in totality in life. Sometimes, despite your best, smart efforts, you fail. Well, then it is just too bad. You cannot succeed every time. Accept it. Don't get disheartened. Take the blame on you like a true leader. Don't blame it to the juniors in your team but blame it to destiny and listen to the good old song 'Que Sera, Sera' by Doris Day on YouTube.

There is a difference in not succeeding and failing. I interpret not succeeding as not getting success but then more attempts are still there, while failure is failing to close the chapter. Also, I believe in the statement 'As we go more and more technology dependent, we start losing more and more on humanity.' I need not elaborate this statement as this is visible to every Tom, Dick, or Harry. Therefore, it is important that although we should keep pace with the advancement of technology, we should not lose track of humanity. Full amount of automation cannot be done by dispensing with the living beings.

I close this book with poetry of Robert Frost which I have been following in my life in true letters:

> The woods are lovely, dark, and deep.
>
> But I have promises to keep, miles to go before I sleep.
>
> And miles to go before I sleep.
